VIOLA
AND THE MINDFUL BUTTERFLY

By Tamarah Teixeira, MA, NCC, LPC, LCPC
Illustrated by Aneeza Ashraf and Ammar Mushtaq

AuthorHouse™
1663 Liberty Drive
Bloomington, IN 47403
www.authorhouse.com
Phone: 833-262-8899

Because of the dynamic nature of the Internet, any web addresses or links contained
in this book may have changed since publication and may no longer be valid. The views
expressed in this work are solely those of the author and do not necessarily reflect the
views of the publisher, and the publisher hereby disclaims any responsibility for them.

Any people depicted in stock imagery provided by Getty Images are models,
and such images are being used for illustrative purposes only.
Certain stock imagery © Getty Images.

This book is printed on acid-free paper.

ISBN: 978-1-6655-0643-4 (sc)
ISBN: 978-1-6655-0644-1 (hc)
ISBN: 978-1-6655-0642-7 (e)

Library of Congress Control Number: 2020921708

Print information available on the last page.

Published by AuthorHouse 12/26/2020

authorHOUSE®

I would like to dedicate this book to my nephews and niece.
Isaac, Adina, and Gabriel Teixeira, you bring happiness to my heart.

A bright sky, the smell of fresh flowers, and a charming soft breeze paved the way for a beautiful day.

Unfortunately, Viola's mind was filled with fear and worry.

"Will I be bullied on the bus again today?" she wondered gloomily. "I can't stand going on Bus 99."

Suddenly Viola heard a voice ask, "What's causing such a pretty girl to look so sad today?"

Confused, Viola looked around to see who was talking to her. No one was near, except for a butterfly. It was the most beautiful butterfly that Viola had ever seen.

"Who said that?" she asked, loudly.

"Over here," said the butterfly.

Viola was astounded. "I must be dreaming," she said to herself. "Butterflies can't talk."

Grace smiled and said, "Well, this is one butterfly who does speak. My name is Grace. I am Grace the energetic, fabulous, fearless, caring, and gorgeous butterfly. I fly around and bring happiness to children by empowering them. I help them to enjoy their day."

"Awesome!" said Viola. "Nice to meet you."

Grace looked intently at Viola and asked, "What's bothering you today?"

Viola sadly replied, "I can't stand going on the bus because the kids bully me. They call me awful names, make fun of my clothes, gossip about my hair, throw things at me, and even push me. The kids on Bus 99 are so mean."

Grace said, "I'm so sorry to hear this. It's not nice when people act aggressively towards us. Viola, I want to help you. Would you like that?"

"How can you help me?" asked Viola. "The kids make me so angry! My heart starts beating very fast when I just think about them."

Grace asked Viola to tell her about a time when she helped to blow up balloons.

"Balloons? What do balloons have to do with this?" asked Viola angrily. "I want the bullying to end!"

"Bullying can be stopped through caring adults like your principal, guidance counselor, teachers, and parents. Even your classmates can help to end school bullying. I want to help you feel good when you walk to the school bus."

Grace began to sing, "Remember to do these three things when you feel angry and sad:

Accept your feelings,

breathe in and breathe out,

take in everything around you."

Amazed, Viola responded, "Wow, you're a great singer, Grace the butterfly!"

"Thank you!" said Grace.

Grace then said in a serious tone, "Now, tell me about a time you helped to blow up balloons."

"Okay," Viola replied, thinking hard. "I remember helping my family to blow up balloons for my little brother's birthday party."

"Birthday party?" said Grace. "Those are always great!"

"Yes, we enjoyed the party. It was so much fun," said Viola happily. "My dad hired a clown who kept us all laughing. Dad also invited a magician who did the most amazing magic tricks. It was the best day."

"Terrific!" said Grace. "Keep that memory in your mind. We will return to it."

"Now, think about what's causing you to feel angry today," said Grace.

Pouting, Viola replied, "Do I have to think about bullying again? Thinking about my little brother's birthday party put me in a much better mood."

"Thoughts of bullying are uncomfortable," agreed Grace in a concerned voice. "I just want to show you how to feel relief. *First*, **accept** your feeling of anger. Where do you feel anger in your body?"

Viola thought about this for a moment, and then answered, "I feel the anger in my heart. Anger makes my heart beat very fast. It makes me upset!"

"When you feel like this, you need to say the following," said Grace to Viola. "*I accept this angry feeling. I'm really upset. I feel this anger in my heart. Yeah, it's not a good feeling. I might feel this anger all day. It's my emotion, and I accept it. Right now, I choose to focus on the moment.*"

"*Secondly,* **breathe in fully**, fill your tummy with air. Hold the air in for 7 seconds. Next breathe out completely, releasing all the air, just like you did when you blew up balloons for your brother's party. Do this step twice more."

Viola did what Grace suggested.

"How do you feel now?" asked Grace.

Viola replied, "Wow, I feel much calmer."

"Great," said Grace. "Do this whenever you have angry or sad thoughts."

"You said there were three steps," Viola reminded Grace. "What's the third one?"

Grace smiled. "**_For the third step_**, you need to use your five senses to concentrate on the moment."

"What do you mean?" asked Viola.

Grace explained, "Think about what you can see, hear, feel, smell, and taste. Try to identify three things from each sense. Continue walking and pay attention to everything around you. It's okay if you become distracted by other thoughts. Allow them to flow through your mind like rain falling from the sky."

As she walked, Viola did as Grace suggested, taking in everything around her and really concentrating with her senses. She hardly realized that 10 minutes had already passed.

"How are you feeling now?" Grace asked.

"I feel a lot better," said Viola, surprised.

"Fantastic," said Grace.

"Another tip to help you during difficult times is using the three strengths," said Grace. "Saying your three strengths will uplift you. For example, I could say: I'm lovely Grace because I am an excellent sister, fabulous artist, and great helper."

Viola listened intently. She wanted to learn more.

Then Grace asked, "What are your strengths? List three things that you are proud of."

"Like what?" asked Viola.

"Like any accomplishment or talent. Anything you do really well."

"Hmmm," thought Viola. Then she said, "I'm smart, friendly, and artistic."

"Great," said Grace, "Now, this is how you use them when you are feeling down. Say, I am _____, I am _____, I am _____,therefore I am amazing."

Viola smiled and repeated, "I am smart, I am friendly, I am artistic, therefore I am amazing!"

Grace faced Viola and said, "It looks like your bus has arrived, here take this."

Grace handed Viola a pocket mirror with stars on it that read, "Who I am matters." She waved to Viola and then flew away.

Viola felt nervous and scared as she stepped onto the bus. But then she remembered Grace singing:

Accept your feelings,

breathe in and breathe out,

take in everything around you.

Viola smiled and felt calmer. She sat down.

 # SCHOOL BUS RULES

*Obey the school bus driver

*Sit properly and remain seated at all times

*Keep head and arms inside the bus

*Do not damage the bus and keep it clean

*Fasten seatbelt

*No yelling, bullying, or fighting

*No profane language

*Do not throw objects

*No cell phone use without permission of driver

*Do not block the aisle

The reader will see page 15 and 16.

Next, the reader will be asked to choose a row to sit in.

Please remember the row you selected.

Rows 6-10

Row 1: Hey Viola, those are cool shoes. (15 points — You communicated a greeting and compliment.)

Row 2: What's poppin'? Would you like to sit here? (20 points — You were friendly/welcoming and initiated a conversation.)

Row 3: Good morning, I like your hairstyle, it's pretty. (15 points — You communicated a greeting and compliment.)

Row 4: It's good to see you today. (15 points — You communicated a friendly, welcoming greeting.)

Row 5: What's Up? (20 points — You communicated a greeting and initiated a conversation.)

Row 6: Ewww, you can't sit here. (0 points – You were rude.)

Row 7: You threw an object. (0 points – You were rude and broke a bus rule.)

Row 8: You chose to use hurtful language (0 points – You were rude.)

Row 9: You disobey a school bus rule (0 points – You broke a bus rule.)

Row 10: Ewww, you can't sit here. You also threw an object. (0 points – You were rude and broke a bus rule.)

CAFETERIA

Cafeteria (Points room)

If you sat in a seat with points, please use your points in the cafeteria.

Principal's Office (No points earned room)

When they arrived at school, all the children who misbehaved on the bus were sent to the principal's office.

In the office stood Ms. Julia (school bus monitor), Mr. Lewis (school principal), and Mr. Kenny (school security guard).

In a firm tone, Mr. Lewis said, "I will not tolerate misbehavior on Bus 99. If you keep misbehaving, I will tell your parents about this and you will be banned from travelling on the bus."

After arriving at school, Viola ate breakfast in the cafeteria. Then she walked to her first class, which was reading. Afterwards, the principal called all the pupils to the auditorium for an important meeting. Viola was nervous because all the teachers looked very serious.

Mr. Lewis said, "Good morning, students and staff. Bullying is a problem here at Flowers Elementary School. But bullying has no place in this school, and we will not allow it to continue. Girls and boys, if you choose to verbally or physically bully your classmates in school or on the bus, your parents will be notified. You will be suspended from school or the bus. Help us to end school bullying. Be kind to each other. During the lunch break, sit next to someone you have not sat next to before. Compliment one another, smile more often. Each child in this school is a shining star. I ask each of you to think about what makes you stand out and shine. What is your talent? How can you use your talent to help a classmate? How can you be kind? Our doors are open if you need to talk about this."

INTIMIDATING

AGGRESSIVE

MEAN

BOTHERSOME

FEARFUL

BOSSY

At the end of the school day, Viola began to feel nervous again. Her heart started beating fast. As she stepped on the bus, Viola remembered what Grace the butterfly taught her: *Accept your feelings, breathe in and breathe out, take in everything around you.*

Viola focused her attention on doing these steps.

Row 1: You smile and say, "What's Up? What are you doing after school?"

Row 2: You offer a greeting.

Row 3: You offer a greeting and start a friendly conversation.

While walking home, Viola thought, "The bus ride home was good today. When the bus arrived, I felt nervous again but I decided to do what Grace taught me:

I accepted my feeling,

I took three deep breaths,

I took in everything around me,

And I ended up feeling much better."

Although Viola did not see Grace on the way home, she was grateful for such a magical encounter.

Bullies are not nice, they are mean.
They try to make fun of you and take your things.
They want to beat you up if you don't share.
Getting what they want is the only thing that makes a bully care.
Bullies are at school, at work, they are everywhere.
A bully is a person who gets mad if you say no.
A bully hides their feelings and tries not to let them show.
If you ever feel you are bullied by someone else, tell a
teacher or an adult and make sure they help.

Aaron R. – Poetically Correct

About the Author

Tamarah Teixeira is a Licensed Clinical Professional Counselor in Maryland. She is a Licensed Professional Counselor in Washington, DC. Tamarah is a National Certified Counselor. She earned a Bachelor of Arts Degree in Psychology from Tuskegee University. Tamarah Teixeira graduated with a Master of Arts Degree in Counseling Psychology from the American School of Professional Psychology (Argosy University). Tamarah has over a decade of experience in the field of Psychological Counseling. She has counseled different cultures, Active Duty Service Members and their children, physically challenged teenagers/adults, and mentally ill adults. Tamarah has facilitated Mindfulness seminars to federal, state, and city government personnel. She believes that lives can be enhanced through counseling support.

Printed in the United States
by Baker & Taylor Publisher Services